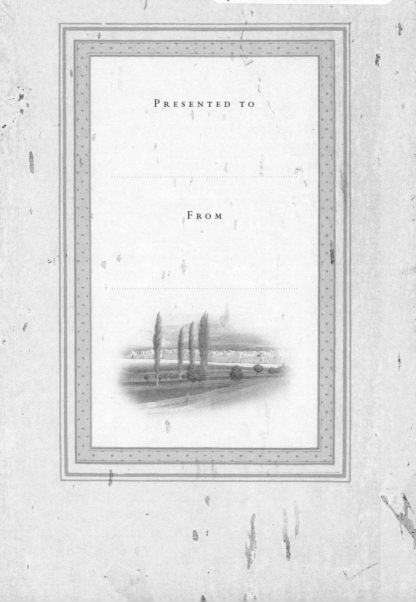

PRESENTED TO

....

FROM

....

THE PRODIGAL'S SISTER

with the art of ROBERT DOARES

JOHN PIPER

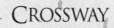

CROSSWAY

A DIVISION OF GOOD NEWS PUBLISHERS

The Prodigal's Sister

Text copyright © 2003 by John Piper

Illustrations by Robert Doares from *Immanuel, God With Us* copyright
© 1994, Crossway Books

Published by Crossway Books *a division of Good News Publishers*

1300 Crescent Street, Wheaton, Illinois 60187

Design by UDG | DesignWorks, www.udgdesignworks.com

First printing 2003

Printed in Italy

LIBRARY OF CONGRESS CATALOGING-IN-PUBLICATION DATA

Piper, John, 1946-
 The prodigal's sister / John Piper
    p. cm.
 ISBN 1-58134-529-1 (alk. paper)
 1. Prodigal son (Parable)--Poetry. 2. Brothers and sisters--Poetry.
I. Title.
 PS3566.I59P56 2003
 811'.54--dc21

                                    2003006926

PBI 11   10   09   08   07   06   05   04   03

13   12   11   10   9   8   7   6   5   4   3   2   1

To All Who
Ever Loved a Prodigal

A Word to the Reader • 9

PART ONE

Both His Sons Had Died • 11

PART TWO

Your Little Girl Can Raise the Dead • 25

PART THREE

May I Please Have This Dance? • 43

A Word to the Reader

Prodigal. I don't know which is harder—to be one or to love one. But I know that when he comes home, there is great joy. Jesus' Parable of the Prodigal Son is about God and how he welcomes sinners who come home through Jesus.

Songs and poems and paintings and prayers have been inspired by this story. But I wonder if anyone has pondered the possibility that besides the prodigal and the older brother, there may have been a daughter. Jesus doesn't say how the prodigal "came to himself." But wouldn't it be just like the ways of God to use the weak things of the world to shame the strong?

Hayaneta is the prodigal's sister. For ten years she has dreamed about finding her brother. Finally the time has come. It is not safe for a beautiful eighteen-year-old girl in the sinful city of Noash. But Hayaneta is no ordinary girl. And before her mission is complete, even her older brother will taste the sway of her courageous love.

John Piper

PART ONE

BOTH HIS SONS
HAD DIED

The road down from the father's farm
Was empty, like an empty arm
That once embraced and then let go,
Or beckoned someone from below.
The road runs west and curves its way
Through miles and miles of wheat, and may,
At harvest time, look like a path
Through paradise, or walls of wrath,
Like water heaped on either side
Of Israel, for one, a tide
To save, and for another, slay.
At first the slope that leads away,
And westward falls, is kind and soft,
Then cursed with falling stones, and oft
With wind and rutted steeps. And so,
It proves an easy way to go,

And hard to come. The front porch of
The mansion, with a roof above
For shade, and rocking chairs below,
Was planned and built ten years ago,
And faces west. And recently
A ramp was added there to free
The old man from the steps. His knees
Had gotten bad.

T he cedar trees,
    Spread 'round the house, cast shadows now
    As Hahyaneta kept her vow,
And sat before her father on
The steps, and prayed that dusk or dawn
Would bring her brother home. The old
Man watched her from his chair, controlled
And measured in the mingling of
His pain and pleasure, with a love,
Perhaps, that only fathers know.
Her brother Manon long ago

Gave up these futile seasons (as
He thought) and worked instead. He had
More fruitful things to do than gaze
With dreamers as the final rays
Of light and hope, he said, fade from
The western sky. His heart was numb
And cold. And so his father cried,
And felt that both his sons had died:
The one from play when passions boil,
The other from his toxic toil.
The one a hundred miles away,
The other even while he stay.
The one a slave to lust and fools,
The other slave to laws and rules.

But Hahyaneta freely came
And nightly watched her brother's name
Fall from her father's silent lips
In prayer, and saw the way it rips
His heart, and learned from him the way
To love. This night her mind would stray
Back to the time ten years ago
And more, when she was eight or so,
And, oh, so happy when they played
With her. Both brothers and the staid
Old man, now sitting in his chair,
Eyes closed and whispering his prayer,
Would lie down in the autumn sheaves
And she would cover them with leaves
And cedar straw. Then she would leap
And clap, as if to wake from sleep,
And there would be a great earthquake,
And three grown men would rise and shake
And shout aloud with arms outspread:
"Our little girl can raise the dead."

And so tonight she pondered this.

At eighteen she still felt the kiss
Of Níqvah on her cheek, ten years
Ago, for one last time, and tears
Ran down his face when she said, "Níq,
Don't go." She hugged his waist. Then quick,
As if to do it while he could,
He turned and ran down through the wood,
So he could stop to cry, then fled
Along the empty road that led
Down to the west away from all
His family and home. A call
That no one understood, and he,
Perhaps, the least, now seemed to be
All-overpowering. His place
Was bare, nor has she seen his face.

Ten years have turned a little lass
Into a woman now. But pass
As time may do, some things do not.
And Hahyaneta's heart for what
One day she planned to do, was just
As sure as on that night she thrust
Her little hand into the dark
And said, "I'll find you, Níqvah! Mark
My words. Someday I'll find you dead
And bring you home alive."

His head
Was lifted now, and eyes were wide
To look once more and see who plied
The road from west to east. At last
She said, "My father, firm and fast,
Like great spikes in a tree, your love
For Níqvah strengthens me above
My every other love, save yours,
And year by year this love endures.

And now I am eighteen, and ask
Your blessing on the only task
That I have dreamed and planned for all
These years that Níq, since I was small,
Has been away. I want to go
And find him where he is, and show
Him he can still come home."

He closed
His weak'ning eyes as if he dozed,
Then said, "Just like your mother spoke,
You speak. She would be pleased to stoke
Your fire and send you on your way
With iron shield and sword to slay
Whatever dragons lay twixt you
And exploits that you aim to do."
He smiled. "But, Hahya, she is gone,
You know. All dragons slain but one:
The fever. She fought well and lost,

And now, my daughter, is the cost
Of having Níqvah, losing you?
It is not safe for girls to do
Such things, or go where Níqvah lives.
I've been there many times. It gives
My heart a shudder just to think
Of how they lust and what they drink
And what they say to girls and do.
Níqvah is not the boy that you
Remember, Hahyaneta. He's
Changed." "Father, I know all of these
Unpleasant things. It's plain to me
That he has changed. But so have we.
Ten years of prayer were not in vain.
And I believe some things remain
From all you've taught, a tender tug,
And that he still can feel the hug
I gave him when he pulled away
Just like I feel his kiss today.

And, Father, most of all, you taught
Me there's a Pow'r in love that naught
Can thwart, and that it moves where truth
And courage speak, and neither youth
Nor age can hinder its success,
But only fear and quietness.
My mother died when I was six
And I still see today the sticks
She broke and said, 'See that! Just so
God breaks the back of ev'ry foe
To bring his children home.' I think
That she would let me go." "A blink,
My daughter, in a blink she would
Have let you go." "And you? I could
Not well succeed without your hand
Of blessing on my head." He scanned
The darkening west and empty road
And fields, and wondered what they bode
Now for his little girl; then raised
His trembling, empty arm and praised

The grace and courage in her heart,
And did then, in these words, impart
A blessing, with his right hand laid
Now gently on her head: "Invade,
My valiant daughter, darkness now,
And I will keep our common vow
Here in this place until you come
Again, and may you bring me some
Good news beyond the gift of men,
That both my boys may live again."

A CALL

O weary soul, with waiting spent,
Cease not to hope, nor cries relent.
And when the months stretch into years
And decades gather up the tears,
Know this, a little girl——or, it
May be, a boy——is being knit,
All by design, in someone's womb
To breathe against the evening gloom,
And then become, in ways that you
Have never dreamed, nor ever knew,
A light within your dark'ning sky,
And answer to your deepest cry.

PART TWO

YOUR LITTLE GIRL CAN RAISE THE DEAD

The old man leaned against the beam
Beside his ramp, and watched a dream
Unfold before his weakened eyes,
And prayed that Hahyaneta's prize
Would be her brother's life. He raised
His empty arm and smiled, amazed
That ten years had not broken the
Resolve and hope in her that she
Would be the way her brother would
Come home. He waved once more, and stood
There on the porch, and watched her take
The final turn from sight, and make
Her lonely way toward Noash on
The coast. He thought, "Your mother's brawn
And beauty mingle well in you,
My child. I know what she would do,

If she were here. She'd look at me
And say, 'It's time to eat.' Then she
Would go inside to spread the meal
And wait for news that Hahya's heel
Had crushed the serpent's head of lies
And freed her son to be the prize
Of Hahyaneta's quest."

The old
Man lingered. Better than he told,
Or wished to tell, he knew the way
To Noash, and the town. The day
Would not go down until some knave
Would hurl a slur against his brave
And tender girl. The road that leads
To Noash is a trap, but breeds,
Against its gluttony and lure,
A grief and anguish in the pure.

Five days she walked, and slept at night
In synagogues, or in the sight
Of one, if rabbis were unsure
That she was scrupulous. The poor
Would take her in and make a place;
And she would say at dawn: "May grace
Abound to you, and would you pray
That very soon my brother may
Receive me in the way you did."
And then she ventured on and bid
Them all farewell, until she came
To Noash by the sea.

The flame
 Above the curving rim of blue
 And rolling waves fell blazing through
The evening haze, and boiled with blood-
Red spray, it seemed, and sent a flood
Of molten crimson flowing forth
On the horizon to the north
And south. She climbed a hill outside
The town so she could watch, and tried
To put herself in Níqvah's place,
And thought: "I wonder if his face
Is ever set to climb this hill,
And watch the west, and feel the thrill
Of what I see: An image of
The heritage our father's love
Bequeaths to us in endless seas

Of golden grain that roll like these
Great waves, and blaze with fire like them
In beauty, but do not condemn
The seamen who embark and fail
But only those who will not sail."
She wondered, as the sun went down,
Where she should stay the night: in town,
Or on a nearby farm? And as
She prayed, she thought, "My father has
A lot of rooms and loves to share.
Perhaps there is a farm somewhere
Nearby with rooms and with a heart
Like his." She raised her head, and part
Way up the hill along the road
An old man with a crooked goad
And scrawny goat walked slowly from
The field, and as he sang a psalm,
Made his way home. His face was thin
And on his neck there was more skin
Than there was meat to fill. She knew
The song. It made her tremble through

The twilight—and rejoice. The man
Must be some distant kin and clan
To know this song. And yet it did
Not bode well for her brother's bid
To live, if wealth had taken wing.
Just barely could she hear him sing:

> "When the staff is broken,*
> And in judgment spoken
> Righteousness is heard,
> Think not God is silent,
> Though the famine violent,
> This is but His word.
> He stands not to give account.
> It is we who must before Him.
> Come, let us adore Him!"

* The song is to the tune of "Jesus Priceless Treasure."

"Excuse me sir, I'm looking for
A place to stay, a simple floor,
Or porch. I have a blanket of
My own. Perhaps a roof above
My head, that's all." The old man gazed
A long time. Then he said, "Amazed;
I am amazed. He said I'd see
And be amazed." "Who said you'd be
Amazed? At what?" "Your father said
I'd be amazed. Well, shake my head!
I truly am amazed! You look
Just like them." "Like who?" Her voice shook.
"Your father and your brother. There,
The chin, the cheek, the nose, the hair.
Amazing." "Sir, which brother do
You mean?" "I mean the one that you
Have come to find, Níqvah." "You know
My brother's name?" "And yours, although
You don't know me. Your given name
Is Hahyaneta. And your fame
Has come before you. He told me

For years that one day I would see
You on the road to Noash. In
Your blood, he said. It's more than skin
That knits you to your mother and,
I add, your father." "Sir, I stand
Before a man I do not know,
And yet who knows me well. Please show
Me who you are, and take me to
My brother."

"Come, let's walk. I knew
Your father years ago when he
First came to seek his son and see
If he could take him home. The lad
Refused, and so your Father bade
Me keep an eye on him, and gave
Me money. 'Keep him from the grave,'
He said. And so for ten years I
Have seen your father come and try,
Time after time, to show the boy

That there is hope and far more joy
At home than in this place. I know
Your father very well." "I owe
You much, kind sir. Tell me, how long
Has famine reigned? I heard the song.
Does Níqvah have enough to pay?"
"The boy eats carob pods to stay
Alive. He steals them from the pigs,
And sometimes gathers flint and twigs
For pennies and a place to stay."
"Do you know where he is today?"
The old man pointed to a shed
With three sides. "There, he makes his bed,
With bats, and sleeps on gathered leaves.

His daily rent: to keep the thieves
Away and feed the swine. I'll wait
Here if you like." "You've been a great
Help, sir, but you don't need to stay.
I'll be all right. Thank you, and may
My father trouble you no more.
Come visit us. My father's door
Is always open." "Fare thee well,
Young lass. It was no trouble. Tell
Your father I will come someday."

She walked down toward the shed. He lay
There on the leaves as still as death.
She wondered, as she watched, if breath
Still came. His eyes were closed. His cheek
Was dark and hollow, and the reek
Was foul. His fingernails were caked
With dirt, and streaks of black soil snaked
Across his rutted brow. His hair
Had not been washed for months. And there
Were no shoes anywhere. His feet
Were bare, his ragged cloak replete
With eaten holes. And in his sleep
He gripped a pouch he used to keep
The parchments that his father sent.
She kneeled beside his head and bent
Down over him and kissed his cheek.
Incredibly there was no shriek
Or sudden jerk. He stared into
The face of Hahyaneta. "Who
Are you?" he said, and sat up in
His leaves. "Hi, Níq. You've gotten thin."

No one had called him Níq for years,
Except his dad. He saw the tears
Pool in her eyes. And then she said,
"Your little girl can raise the dead."
His mouth fell open. "Hahya?" "Yes,
I said I'd come, no more no less,
And bring you home, alive." "The last
Time I saw you, you hadn't passed
Four feet. You must be eighteen now."
He pushed the hair back from her brow.
"It's really you. Did you come by
Yourself?" "Yes." "Why? You want to die?
This city is a pit. It blinds
The young with dazzling names, then binds
And swallows them alive." "I'm here,
To bring you home," she said, "it's clear
You don't belong." "As clear as mud.
Look, Hahya, you don't know the crud
Inside. You don't know who I am."
"Hear this, my brother, I do damn
Those words and call them lies. It's you

Who don't know who you are. It's true
There is a mystery. What makes
You think the dazzled dupes and fakes
Of Noash can declare the true
And wonderful design of who
You are? One knows, and only one,
Who Níqvah is. And when you're done
With dabbling in the darkness here –
All dazzling as it is—the clear,
Bright air of eastern skies will bring
You home to him. And I will sing.
Awake, O sleeper, from the grave,
You are a son and not a slave."

They sat in silence for a long
Long time. He was amazed how strong
This little girl of eight had grown.
And then she changed her look and tone:
"He built a porch just after you
Had left. It faces west. We knew
What it was for. He'll be there, Níq.
And will not quench a smoldering wick.
Come home with me. Even tonight.
I have some bread, the moon is bright.
It's cooler in the dark, and we
Can sleep by day. Please, come with me."
And quietly the fetters and
The folly fell. She took his hand,
And where he had before said No
A hundred times, he said, "Let's go."

A CALL

Come, flick'ring hope, and carry fire;
From this my story and desire,
Ignite your smold'ring wick, and make
Your candle blaze. And may Christ take
This happy flame and with it burn
Up ev'ry hopeless word, and turn
The fatal dream of false despair
Into the bright and living air
That blows down from the Father's farm.
And may you feel the mighty arm
Of God lift you into the light
Of Truth, and put an end to night.
We do not know ourselves aright
Until we have the Father's light.
We think we know ourselves and groan,
Until we know as we are known.

PART THREE

MAY I PLEASE HAVE THIS HAVE THIS DANCE?

Four nights they walked, and slept by day.
Beneath the carob branches lay
The daughter fast asleep from hard
And weary nights; and keeping guard
Beside her, lay the prodigal,
His moving lips inaudible,
Still restless and awake, transfixed
On bloody bark and branches twixt
The earth and sky, where traitors used
To hang with common thieves accused
Of treason toward their sovereign king
And, in the act, of plundering
His wealth.

The lips of Níqvah spoke
A wordless speech: "O, Father, cloak
This worse-than-naked son with rags,
And feed me from the garbage bags,
And let me live with slaves, for I
Have treated you with scorn, and my
Contempt was worse than all the blame
That stained this bloody tree with shame,
Which now, with life and leaves arrayed,
Spreads out and covers me with shade.
I do not ask to sit with kings,
But only shade beneath your wings."

And so the prodigal rehearsed
His speech and waited for the first
Signs of his sister's wakening.
Mid afternoon she stirred. "I'll bring
You water, if you like," he said.
"I'd like that, Níqvah. All the bread
Is gone, you know." "I know. Let's try
To make it home tonight. The sky
Looks happy to the west. I think
We'll make it. I'll go get your drink."
When he returned, the packs were rolled
And Hahyaneta said, "I told
Your brother you would come." "What did
He say?" But Hahyaneta hid
Her face as they began to walk,
And didn't answer him. "Some talk
Of pain is good, you know." "I know.
He said he didn't care. 'Just go
And waste your breath,' he said." The tears
Rolled down her cheeks. "How many years
Has Manon felt that way?" he asked.

"Unless he's keeping something masked,
He never cared." "I'm not surprised.
He never wrote. To be despised
Is sometimes good for us. I don't
Deserve his pity, and I won't
Demand his love. The way I spurned
Our Father surely has well earned
For me whatever Manon feels.
How great his love must be that reels
With hate so long! Perhaps, if he
Believed that I have come to see
How precious is our Father's care
And how unspeakable and rare
His heart, and noble is his mind,
Then, maybe, there would be a kind
Of softening of Manon toward
My soul." "I wish for such reward,
My brother, but I fear the wrath
Of Manon grows along a path
Far diff'rent from the one you hope.
Oh, that his anger were the scope

And measure of his love for all
That our great Father is. But gall
And bitterness are not born from
The thrall of mercy nor do come
From treasuring the fountain of
Delight we call our Father's love.
There is another stream that feeds
The bitterness of his good deeds."

Now as the evening came and they
Began to climb the rugged way
That leads up to the great Plateau,
All conversation ceased. Below,
And now behind these two, ten years
Of emptiness burst, to the cheers
Of every waving stalk of grain,
A bubble in the wind, and feign
The beauty it possessed before
It broke. His back now to the shore
Beyond the western rim, the son
Stood trembling on the road—the one
Where he had run the other way,
As though it were but yesterday.
Before him lay what seemed a sea
Of endless gold. What enemy,
He thought, could make a boy believe
That any distant world could weave
A better beauty than this place?
Then suddenly he said, "My face,
My hair! I'm filthy, Hahya. Look

At me!" She smiled at him and took
A long, deep breath, and said, "Let's go."

The old man's chair rocked to and fro.
His lips moved silently as though
He sang some favorite psalm. The glow
Of golden red and crimson rays
Had set the western fields ablaze,
As if some cosmic cause were found
For merry-making. But no sound
Was heard except the rhythm of
The rocking chair. And then, above
The rail, the old man saw two shapes,
And stopped. He thought, "I know the capes
That Hahyaneta wears." He took
The rail and stood so he could look.

And then he saw her lift her hand
The way she always did, then stand,
And let the other shape go on.
He knew. For all his soul was drawn,
And there was no resisting this.
He left his cane, and, lest he miss
A step, he jumped them all, and ran,
Forgetting that he was a man
Of dignity, and that his knees
Were bad. He often thought, with ease
Someday I'll run on these, and more.
Is this not what they're ruined for?

He stopped just long enough to see
His eyes and take a breath. Then he
Embraced the boy, and pressed his face
Against the foul and crusty place
He used to kiss the lad goodnight,
And pushed his fingers through the tight
And matted hair; and there with plain
And heaving sobs, released the pain
Built up four thousand nights. And then,
The weeping son said, "Father, can
Perhaps, you make a slave of me,
For I have sinned and cannot be
Your son?" To which the great old man
Replied, "I have a different plan."
And then, to servants gathered by,
He said, "Bring me the ring, and my
Best robe, and leather shoes. And take
The fire and fatted calf, and make

For us the finest feast that we
Have ever made. For this, you see,
My dead son is alive and sound;
He once was lost, but now is found."
And so the common labor ceased,
And ev'ry hand prepared the feast.
The colors flew at ev'ry gate!
And they began to celebrate.

As usual, Manon was in
The field and working late. He'd been
There since the crack of dawn and worked
All day. "Let duty not be shirked,"
He liked to say, and took some pride
In his long hours, and liked to chide
The servants, that he could out-serve
Them ev'ry day, and out-deserve
Them all. He heard the music from
The house and saw the servants come
Out dancing on the lawn. His first
Response to songs and joy: a burst
Of anger: this is not the way
To serve their Lord! What holiday
Have they declared to frolic like
A carefree child? If I must strike
Them, then I will, to see that they
Learn how to serve and to obey.

"What's all this racket here?" He snapped.
A servant overflowed and clapped,
"He's back! He's back! Níqvah is back!"
He frowned, "And in the prison shack
With other thieves, may I suppose?"
"Oh, no, Sir Manon! Master chose
The fattest calf and killed it for
A feast, and said, 'Bring wine and pour
A goblet for my son, and let
All work be put aside and get
My ring and finest robe with joy,
And put them on my living boy.'"

The older son was stunned and stood
There by the fence he'd made, and would
Not enter. Then his Father saw
Him by the fence, and went to draw
Him in. "Your brother's home. Come see
Him, Manny. He has changed. You'll be
Amazed." "I'll tell you, Father, what
Amazes me: that he can strut
Here like an honored guest although
He took your hard-earned cash to throw
It down the sewers of Noash,
And let you subsidize his brash
And wicked reveling with whores.
And made you weep behind those doors
For ten years while I slaved to make
A profit on this place. So take
Your pick, my Lord, the wicked one
In there, or me, the working son."

"I'd like to think that all these years
You have enjoyed the place. It sears
The soul, Manon, to take your rage
To bed night after night. You wage
A war against your self. Beware
Of other mistresses whose snare
Is just as deadly as the kind
Your brother sought. Oh, be not blind,
My son. All that I have is yours,
And free. For all time it endures.
But if what you desire is pay,
Bequests will never come that way.
Come join me at the table, son,
The labors of the day are done."

But Manon stood there like a stone,
And sent his Father back alone.
The girl was watching from the door,
And as her Father passed, "Once more,
Perhaps," he took her hand and said,
"Our little girl can raise the dead."

She turned and saw the shining face
Of Níqvah laughing in the grace
Of life, then through the evening shade
Beyond the fence that Manon made,
She walked.

His face was streaked where sweat
Ran through the pollen dust, and met
His tangled beard. The garments that
He wore for working stank. And at
The middle of his fingers there
Were blisters on both hands. Despair
Seemed written on his frozen face.
"In vain," he thought. "He said the race
And pace were all in vain. The hours,
The years, the sweat, the plans, my pow'rs—
For naught. Bequests don't come that way."
Then Hahyaneta kissed the gray
And brownish coating on his cheek,
And said, "Hi, Manny. You look weak.
Can I get you a drink?" He shook
His head, "No thanks." "Manon, it took

Your breath away, what Father said.
I think I understand. The dread
You feel right now—that all your sweat
Has been in vain—it's true. And yet
It is a gift to know bequests
Are free, and loaded treasure chests
Of grace, all hidden in the ground,
Are never earned, but only found.
And dancing doesn't come that way,
And happy parties are not pay.
Day labor is of no avail,
The gift of joy is not for sale.
You've labored hard to shun what's bad
And now it's hard to just be glad.

But, Manny, look. Your Father and
The servants and your brother stand
Inside the door and bid you come.
And listen to the children drum!"
She took his hand: "Come, all is well."
And thus the fetters broke and fell.
He waked as from a life-long trance,
And said, "May I please have this dance?"

A CALL

And now, O Christ, let there be light
So we can see the way aright
Between two dismal forms of death,
And with that light, O give us breath
To live again, and bring us back
From pleasures in a foreign shack,
Or from the pride of weary arm,
While working on the Father's farm.
From demon sloth and pleasures raw,
Or demon toil and pride of law.
The pathway home from either place
Is opened by the word of grace.
O Christ, pursue us till we see
That all of God's bequests are free.
The ticket that we have to show
Is this: that we are glad to go.